This List Journal Belongs To

_____

List Journal

50 Lists That Define Me

Table of Contents

Page

Introduction

Keeping lists is a powerful way of getting to know yourself and really drilling down on the things that make you tick. This List Journal has been designed with 50 key questions in mind.

The questions act as prompts to guide you towards self-realisation and also serve to get your thoughts organized all in one place.

The journal will help you to finally open up to yourself with some of the questions allowing you dig deep. Other questions are designed for you to use as placeholders for some of your most important memories and thoughts.

Start your list journal today and organize your mind.

Things I'm Grateful For

What I Love About Myself

Words That Describe Me

Most Positive Memories From My Childhood

My Closest Friends

My Dreams as a Kid

Goals I Want To Achieve

Favorite Songs of All Time

Favorite TV Shows

Favorite Lyrics From Songs

Favorite Quotes

More Favorite Quotes

Best Books I've Read

Books I Want To Read

Movies I Love

Countries I want To Visit

People I Want To Meet

I Want To Be Known For

What Moves Me

Habits I Want To Develop

Things I Want To Change in My Life

Favorite Websites & Blogs

Words I Love & Their Meanings

The Best Advice I Have Ever Received

Things I Like To Do

I Want To Learn To....

Things I'm Worried About

Things That Inspire Me

Favorite Recipes

Favorite Poems

Favorite Restaurants & Types of Food

My Most Treasured Possessions

Things I Will Never Forget

Write About My Favorite Teacher(s)

My Greatest Strengths

My Biggest Weaknesses

My Proudest Moments

Things People Don't Know About Me

Who I Am In Love With and Why

I Like To Shop At:

My Guilty Pleasures

<u>Biggest Challenges in My Life</u>

Things I Feel Most Strongly About

List Some Things To Do When I'm Bored

Best YouTube Channels

The Things I'd Do If Money Were No Object

Things I'm Really Good At

51

My Favorite Hobbies

What Makes Me Different To Most People

Need another List Journal?

Visit www.blankbooksnjournals.com

77484977R00033

Made in the USA
Lexington, KY
27 December 2017